THE
SIMPLE PLEASURES
OF THE
CHRISTIAN LIFE

THE
SIMPLE PLEASURES
OF THE
CHRISTIAN LIFE

Jeanie Price

Star Song Publishing Group
a division of Jubilee Communications, Inc.
P.O. Box 150009
Nashville, Tennessee 37215

ISBN # 1-56233-088-8

Printed in the United States of America
First Printing, September 1993

1 2 3 4 5 6 7 8 9 – 97 96 95 94 93

INTRODUCTION

For over 36 years my father has been a minister. When I was a little girl we didn't have a lot of material possessions but our home was filled with love and laughter and the abiding richness of God's presence.

I remember one Christmas when we lived in Ottumwa, Iowa where my father was the pastor of the First Church of the Nazarene. As usual my sister and I eagerly awaited the festivities of the season and the traditions we enjoyed: reading the Christmas story, the Christmas Eve candle-light service, getting that one special gift we had been dropping hints about since the middle of summer.

That year, however, my mother decided to treat us with a little something extra. I'll never forget the snowy morning when she left early to go shopping and brought home a large box that contained what would become a cherished family memory. It wasn't a sled or a bicycle or an oversized doll house. In fact, it was the last thing we expected.

Inside that brown cardboard box were more pieces of cardboard—only these were gaily colored and looked like . . . bricks. Yes, bricks. And underneath were cardboard logs, and a cardboard mantle, and, finally, cardboard fire! Our small parsonage was filled with the warmth of the holidays but it was missing, my mother decided, that one attribute that was featured on the cover of almost every Christmas card, holiday catalog, and seasonal book: a fireplace. And now we had one too!

My father quickly attached each piece and soon we were sitting beside a roaring 40 watt lightbulb. The glow it cast on our smiling faces reflected the peace and contentment we felt in our hearts knowing that we were warm and safe inside a home filled with happiness and love.

That was over two decades ago and the Lord has since blessed each member of my family in ways that we could not then have imagined. Yet when I think back over memorable events in my life it is always the simple pleasures that stand out. Simple pleasures like that first evening when my family sat around our new fireplace and enjoyed just being together. It may have only cost a few dollars, and has long since fallen apart, but its value has been immeasurable and its impact timeless in terms of the memories it created.

Today I repeatedly hear people say that they would be happy if only they had a more prestigious job or if they just owned a nicer car or if next year they could afford to go to an exotic island on their vacation. Sadly I even hear comments like this from men and women who sit in church pews each Sunday and who hold in their hands the secrets to eternal peace and happiness: the Holy Word of God.

This book is filled with simple words and easy to understand concepts that any child can quickly grasp. Yet each, in its simplicity, has the ability to transform your life and bring you pleasure that no earthly possession can offer or that you could ever afford.

As a child my mother gave our family a simple gift that was significant because of the love it represented. As an adult the single most important gift that my Heavenly Father offers me—offers to anyone who trusts in Him—is the daily pleasure of a holy life in His presence.

Your friend in Christ Jesus,

JEANIE PRICE
Nashville, Tennessee

Love!

THE LORD IS
EXTRAVAGENT WITH HIS LOVE
FOR THOSE
WHO OBEY AND HONOR HIM.

—from Exodus 20:6

Sabbath!

THE LORD HAS GIVEN YOU
A DAY OF REST, THE SABBATH, SO YOU CAN BE
PHYSICALLY AND SPIRITUALLY
REFRESHED FOR THE WEEK AHEAD.

—from Exodus 20:8-10

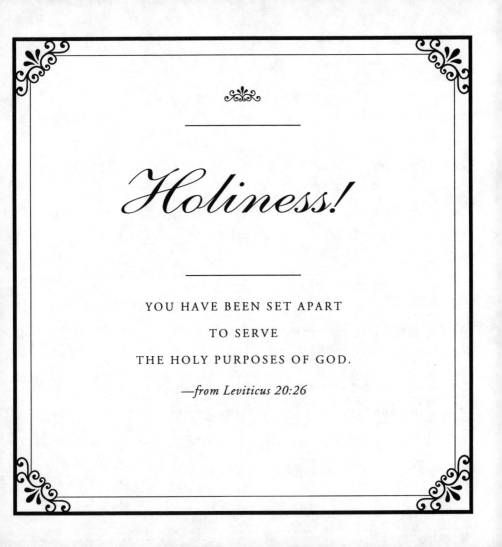

Holiness!

YOU HAVE BEEN SET APART

TO SERVE

THE HOLY PURPOSES OF GOD.

—from Leviticus 20:26

Blessings!

THE BLESSINGS OF THE LORD ARE
GREAT IN NUMBER FOR THOSE WHO SERVE HIM:
BLESSINGS IN YOUR COMMUNITY;
BLESSINGS IN YOUR JOB; BLESSINGS IN YOUR FAMILY;
BLESSINGS IN ALL THAT YOU DO AT HOME
AND IN THE WORLD.

—from Deuteronomy 28:2-6

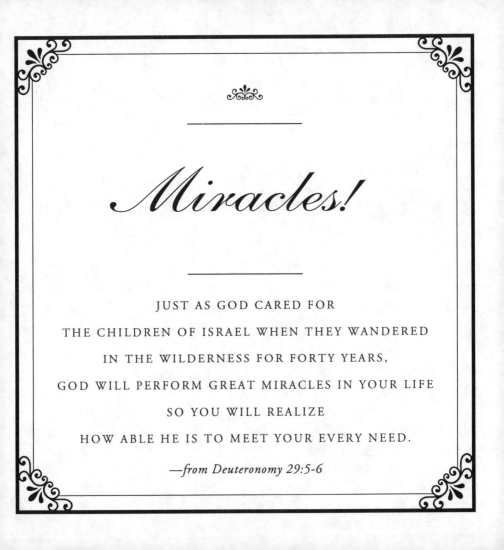

Miracles!

JUST AS GOD CARED FOR
THE CHILDREN OF ISRAEL WHEN THEY WANDERED
IN THE WILDERNESS FOR FORTY YEARS,
GOD WILL PERFORM GREAT MIRACLES IN YOUR LIFE
SO YOU WILL REALIZE
HOW ABLE HE IS TO MEET YOUR EVERY NEED.

—from Deuteronomy 29:5-6

Success!

IF YOU TRUST IN THE LORD
AND BELIEVE IN THOSE
WHO SERVE HIM YOU WILL HAVE GREAT
SUCCESS IN LIFE.

—from 2 Chronicles 20:20

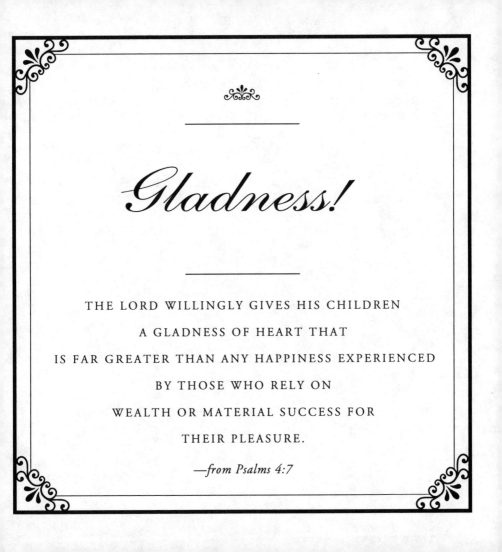

Gladness!

THE LORD WILLINGLY GIVES HIS CHILDREN

A GLADNESS OF HEART THAT

IS FAR GREATER THAN ANY HAPPINESS EXPERIENCED

BY THOSE WHO RELY ON

WEALTH OR MATERIAL SUCCESS FOR

THEIR PLEASURE.

—from Psalms 4:7

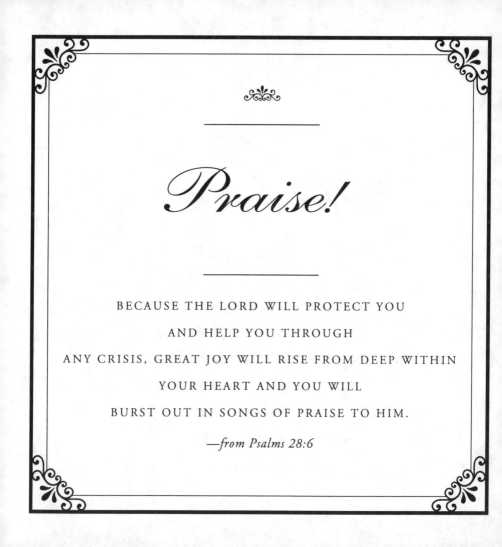

Praise!

BECAUSE THE LORD WILL PROTECT YOU
AND HELP YOU THROUGH
ANY CRISIS, GREAT JOY WILL RISE FROM DEEP WITHIN
YOUR HEART AND YOU WILL
BURST OUT IN SONGS OF PRAISE TO HIM.

—from Psalms 28:6

Protection!

THE LORD PROTECTS THOSE WHO
HONOR HIS WORD AND
BRINGS SUCCESS TO LEADERS WHO HAVE
HIS BLESSING.

—from Psalms 28:8

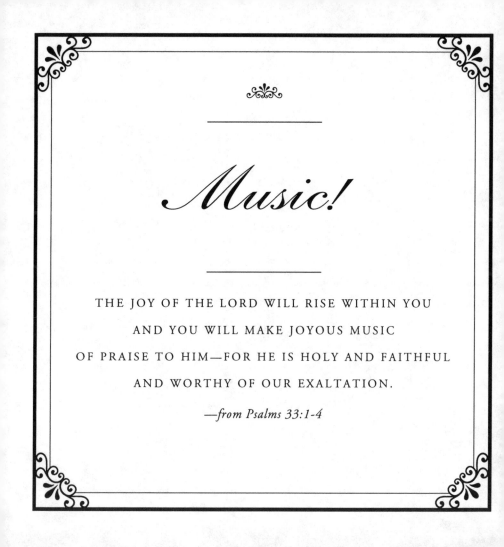

Music!

THE JOY OF THE LORD WILL RISE WITHIN YOU

AND YOU WILL MAKE JOYOUS MUSIC

OF PRAISE TO HIM—FOR HE IS HOLY AND FAITHFUL

AND WORTHY OF OUR EXALTATION.

—from Psalms 33:1-4

Guardian Angels!

THE GUARDIAN ANGELS OF THE LORD

PROTECT AND KEEP

THOSE WHO REVERE HIS NAME.

—from Psalms 34:7

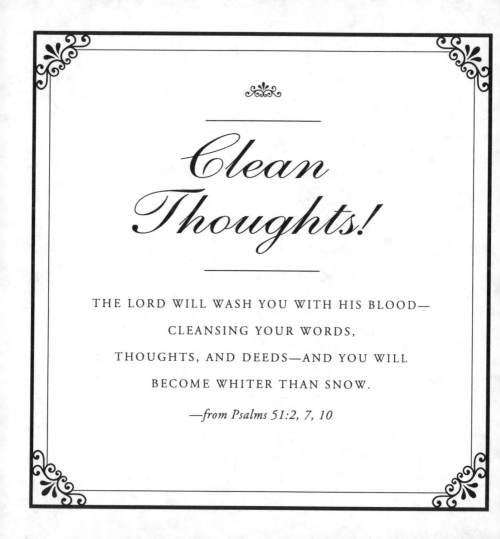

Clean Thoughts!

THE LORD WILL WASH YOU WITH HIS BLOOD—

CLEANSING YOUR WORDS,

THOUGHTS, AND DEEDS—AND YOU WILL

BECOME WHITER THAN SNOW.

—from Psalms 51:2, 7, 10

Thankfulness!

THANK THE LORD FOR ALL THAT HE HAS
DONE FOR YOU:
HE HAS REDEEMED YOU . . . HE HAS SHOWN LOVING
KINDNESS TOWARD YOU . . .
HE HAS PERFORMED NUMEROUS MIRACLES
IN YOUR LIFE.

—from Psalms 107:1-2, 15, 22

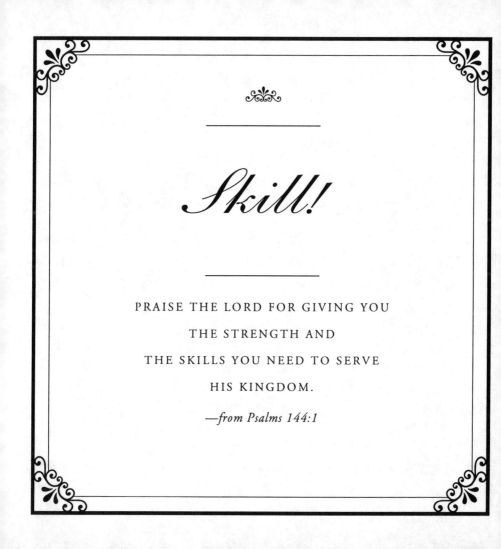

Skill!

PRAISE THE LORD FOR GIVING YOU

THE STRENGTH AND

THE SKILLS YOU NEED TO SERVE

HIS KINGDOM.

—from Psalms 144:1

Compassion!

THE LORD, YOUR GOD IS KIND, MERCIFUL,

SLOW TO ANGER, AND

SHOWS COMPASSION TO EVERYONE.

—*from Psalms 145:8-9*

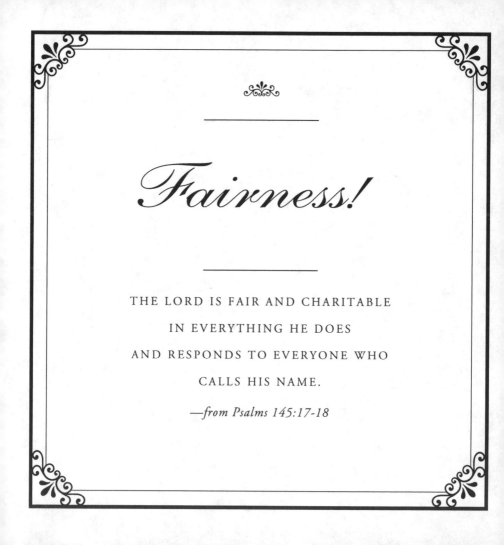

Fairness!

THE LORD IS FAIR AND CHARITABLE

IN EVERYTHING HE DOES

AND RESPONDS TO EVERYONE WHO

CALLS HIS NAME.

—from Psalms 145:17-18

Healing!

THE LORD WILL HEAL YOUR BROKEN HEART

AND BIND ANY

EMOTIONAL WOUNDS YOU MAY HAVE.

—from Psalms 147:3

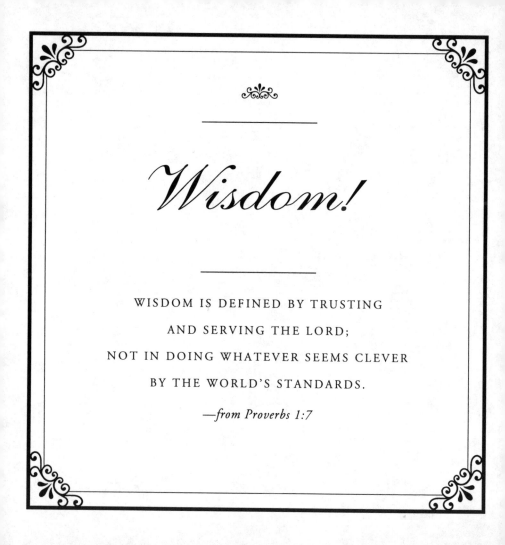

Wisdom!

WISDOM IS DEFINED BY TRUSTING
AND SERVING THE LORD;
NOT IN DOING WHATEVER SEEMS CLEVER
BY THE WORLD'S STANDARDS.

—from Proverbs 1:7

Discernment!

IF YOU VALUE INSIGHT AND DISCERNMENT

ABOVE ALL OTHER ATTRIBUTES,

THEN GOD WILL GIVE YOU TREMENDOUS WISDOM,

AND YOU WILL SOON LEARN

THE IMPORTANCE OF REVERING AND TRUSTING

IN THE LORD.

—from Proverbs 2:3-5

Direction!

GOD WILL DIRECT YOUR STEPS AND
GIVE YOU SUCCESS IN ALL
YOUR EFFORTS IF YOU WILL SIMPLY PLACE HIM
FIRST IN YOUR LIFE.

—from Proverbs 3:6

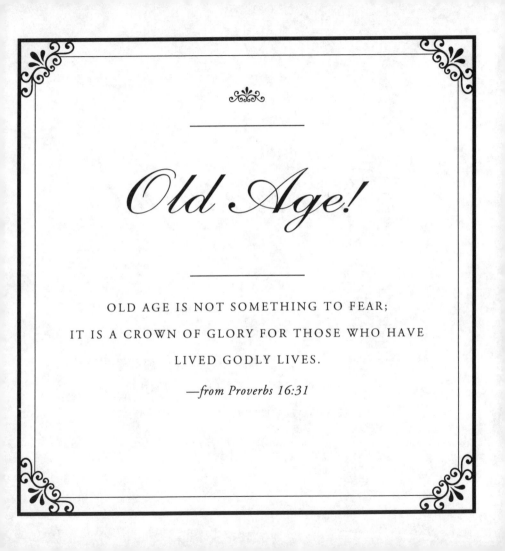

Old Age!

OLD AGE IS NOT SOMETHING TO FEAR;
IT IS A CROWN OF GLORY FOR THOSE WHO HAVE
LIVED GODLY LIVES.

—from Proverbs 16:31

Friendship!

A "FAIR-WEATHER" FRIEND WILL LEAVE YOU

WHEN TIMES ARE TOUGH

BUT YOUR CHRISTIAN BROTHERS AND SISTER WILL

STAY WITH YOU THROUGH

THE GOOD TIMES AND THE BAD.

—*from Proverbs 18:24*

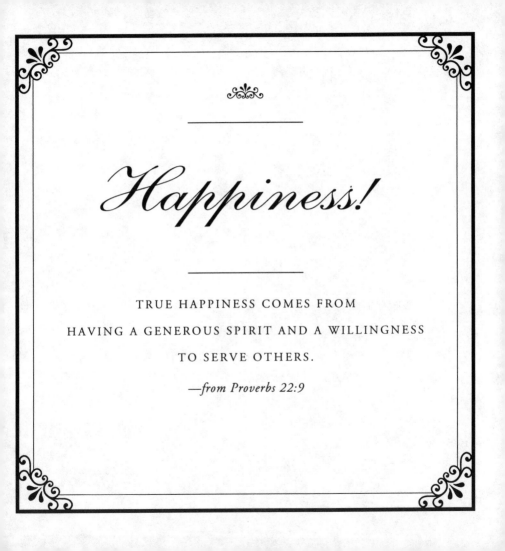

Happiness!

TRUE HAPPINESS COMES FROM
HAVING A GENEROUS SPIRIT AND A WILLINGNESS
TO SERVE OTHERS.

—from Proverbs 22:9

Peace!

GOD'S PEOPLE EXPERIENCE PERFECT PEACE

IN LIFE WHEN

THEY TRUST AND OBEY HIM.

—from Isaiah 26:3

Benevolence!

THE LORD SHINES HIS INFINITE BENEVOLENCE

ON HIS CHILDREN BY GUIDING

THEIR STEPS THROUGHOUT LIFE AND BLESSING

THEM WITH HIS ABUNDANT GOODNESS.

—from Isaiah 58:11

Comfort!

GOD OFFERS COMFORT AND JOY
TO HIS PEOPLE AND PROTECTS THEM FROM
THE UNJUST AND SINFUL
ATTITUDES AND ACTIONS OF UNBELIEVERS.

—*from Isaiah 51:12*

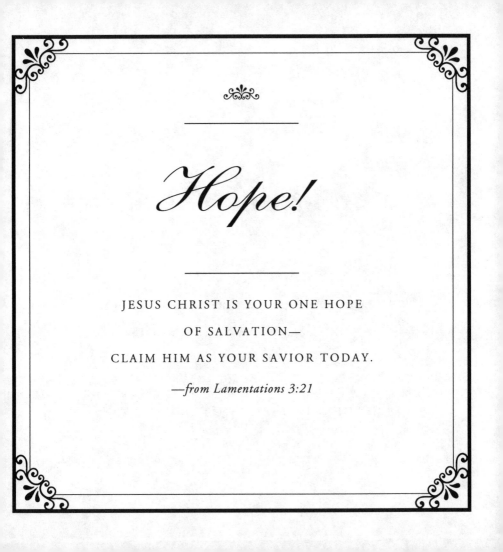

Hope!

JESUS CHRIST IS YOUR ONE HOPE

OF SALVATION—

CLAIM HIM AS YOUR SAVIOR TODAY.

—from Lamentations 3:21

Revelation!

THE LORD WILL GLADLY REVEAL THAT WHICH

IS BEYOND OUR UNDERSTANDING

TO THOSE WHO FAITHFULLY SERVE HIM, FOR HE

KNOWS ALL THE

HIDDEN MYSTERIES OF THE UNIVERSE.

—from Daniel 2:22

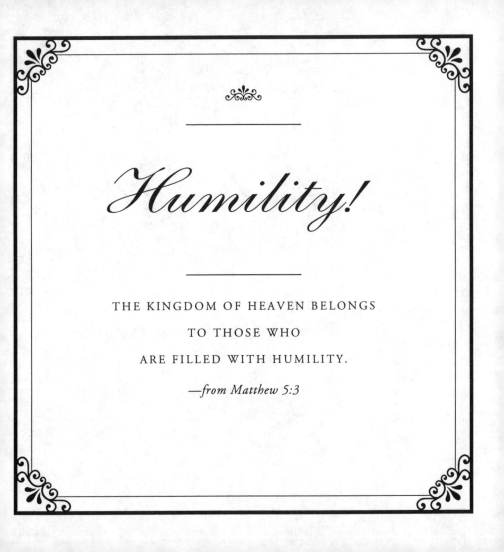

Humility!

THE KINGDOM OF HEAVEN BELONGS

TO THOSE WHO

ARE FILLED WITH HUMILITY.

—from Matthew 5:3

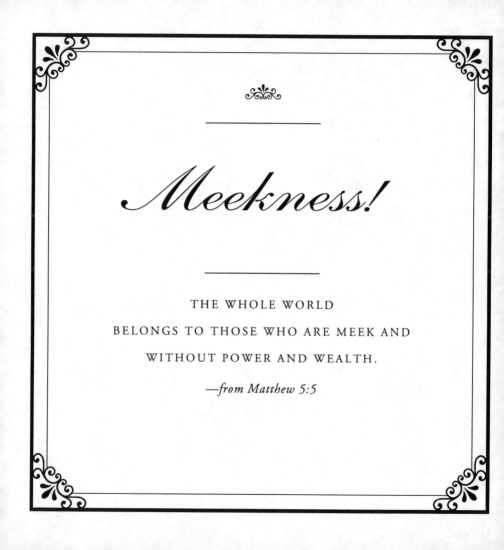

Meekness!

THE WHOLE WORLD

BELONGS TO THOSE WHO ARE MEEK AND

WITHOUT POWER AND WEALTH.

—*from Matthew 5:5*

Perfection!

YOU WILL ALWAYS BE HAPPY AND SATISFIED

IF YOU STRIVE TO BE PERFECT,

JUST AS YOUR FATHER IN HEAVEN IS PERFECT.

—from Matthew 5:6-7

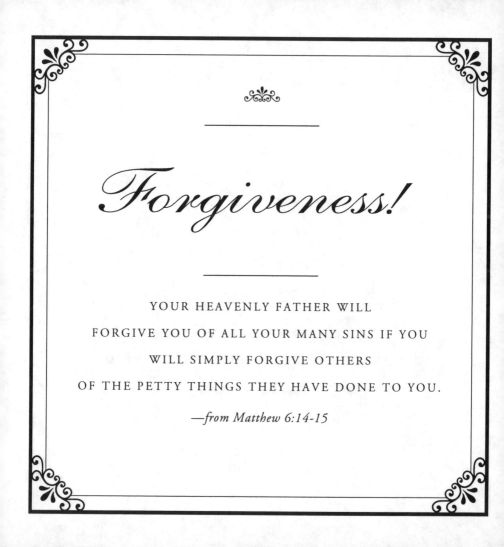

Forgiveness!

YOUR HEAVENLY FATHER WILL
FORGIVE YOU OF ALL YOUR MANY SINS IF YOU
WILL SIMPLY FORGIVE OTHERS
OF THE PETTY THINGS THEY HAVE DONE TO YOU.

—from Matthew 6:14-15

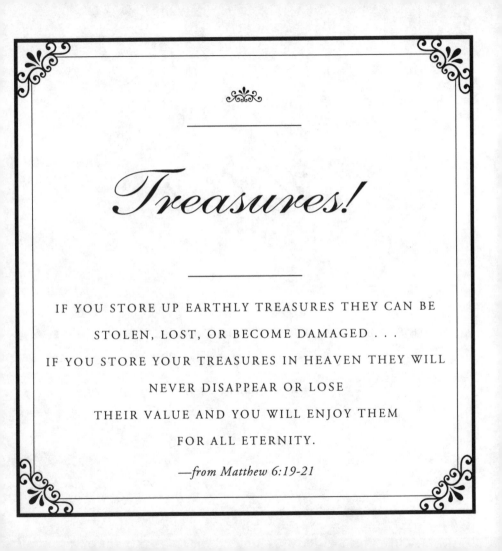

Treasures!

IF YOU STORE UP EARTHLY TREASURES THEY CAN BE

STOLEN, LOST, OR BECOME DAMAGED . . .

IF YOU STORE YOUR TREASURES IN HEAVEN THEY WILL

NEVER DISAPPEAR OR LOSE

THEIR VALUE AND YOU WILL ENJOY THEM

FOR ALL ETERNITY.

—from Matthew 6:19-21

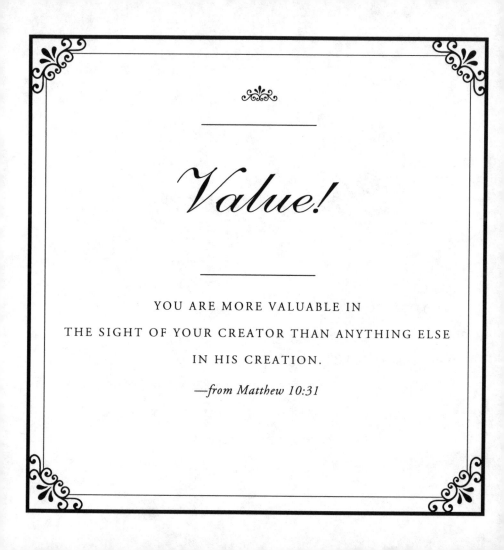

Value!

YOU ARE MORE VALUABLE IN
THE SIGHT OF YOUR CREATOR THAN ANYTHING ELSE
IN HIS CREATION.

—from Matthew 10:31

Rest!

WHEN YOU WORK FOR THE LORD

HE WILL TREAT YOU WITH GREAT CARE AND WILL

OFFER YOU REST

WHEN YOU BECOME WEARY.

—*from Matthew 11:29*

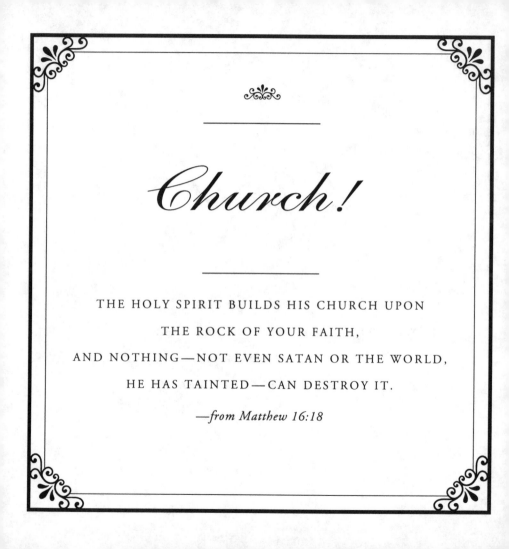

Church!

THE HOLY SPIRIT BUILDS HIS CHURCH UPON
THE ROCK OF YOUR FAITH,
AND NOTHING—NOT EVEN SATAN OR THE WORLD,
HE HAS TAINTED—CAN DESTROY IT.

—from Matthew 16:18

Resurrection!

ON THE DAY OF RESURRECTION THE LORD WILL
SEND HIS ANGELS TO
THE FARTHEST REACHES OF HEAVEN AND EARTH,
GATHERING TOGETHER THOSE WHO
HAVE FAITHFULLY LOVED AND SERVED HIM FOR A
GLORIOUS AND ETERNAL CELEBRATION.

—from Matthew 24:31

Preaching!

AS A CHRISTIAN YOU CAN BE A PREACHER
OF THE GOSPEL AND SHARE
THE GOOD NEWS OF SALVATION WITH YOUR FAMILY,
FRIENDS, AND NEIGHBORS.

—*from Mark 16:15*

Good Deeds!

JUST AS A WICKED HEART IS REVEALED THROUGH
A PERSON'S EVIL WORDS AND ACTIONS, SO,
TOO, WILL YOU DEMONSTRATE THE RIGHTEOUSNESS
GOD HAS PLACED WITHIN YOU
BY CONTINUALLY DOING GOOD DEEDS.

—from Luke 6:45

Rebirth!

IF YOU BELIEVE THAT JESUS HAS CONQUERED
SIN AND DEATH AND THAT
THROUGH HIM YOU WILL HAVE ETERNAL LIFE,
THEN YOU WILL BE
GLORIOUSLY REBORN AND WILL RECEIVE HIS
RICH AND ABUNDANT BLESSINGS.

—from John 1:4

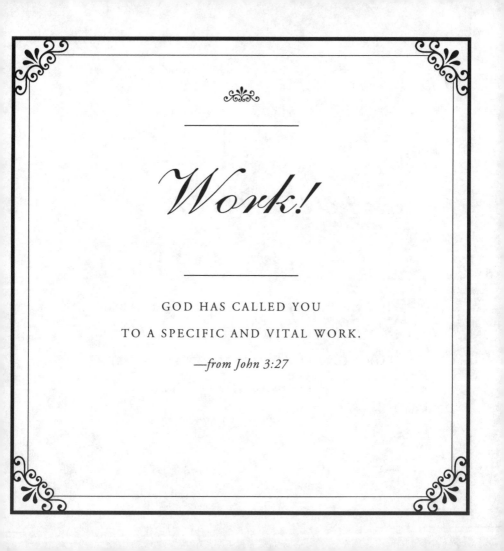

Work!

GOD HAS CALLED YOU
TO A SPECIFIC AND VITAL WORK.

—from John 3:27

Abundance!

THE LIVING WATERS OF THE LORD ARE ABUNDANT
AND WILL QUENCH YOUR THIRST
FOR SALVATION AND SUPPLY YOUR NEEDS
THROUGHOUT ETERNITY.

—from John 4:10-14

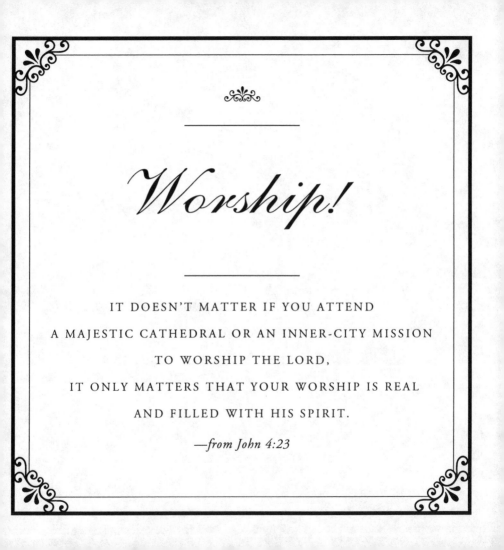

Worship!

IT DOESN'T MATTER IF YOU ATTEND
A MAJESTIC CATHEDRAL OR AN INNER-CITY MISSION
TO WORSHIP THE LORD,
IT ONLY MATTERS THAT YOUR WORSHIP IS REAL
AND FILLED WITH HIS SPIRIT.

—from John 4:23

Nourishment!

JESUS CHRIST IS THE LIVING BREAD AND,

BY HIS REDEEMING POWER,

HE WILL NOURISH YOUR SOUL FOR ETERNITY.

—from John 6:51

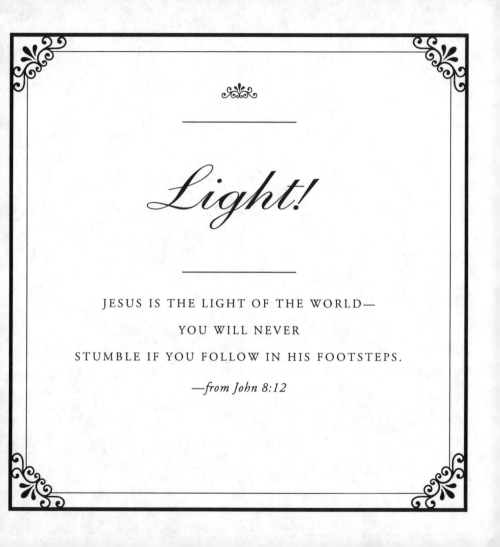

Light!

JESUS IS THE LIGHT OF THE WORLD—

YOU WILL NEVER

STUMBLE IF YOU FOLLOW IN HIS FOOTSTEPS.

—from John 8:12

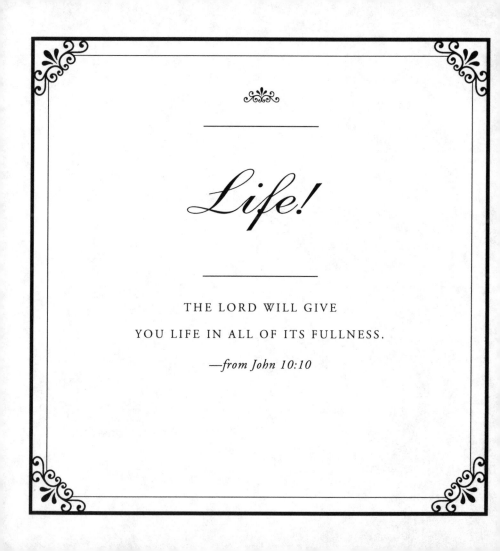

Life!

THE LORD WILL GIVE

YOU LIFE IN ALL OF ITS FULLNESS.

—*from John 10:10*

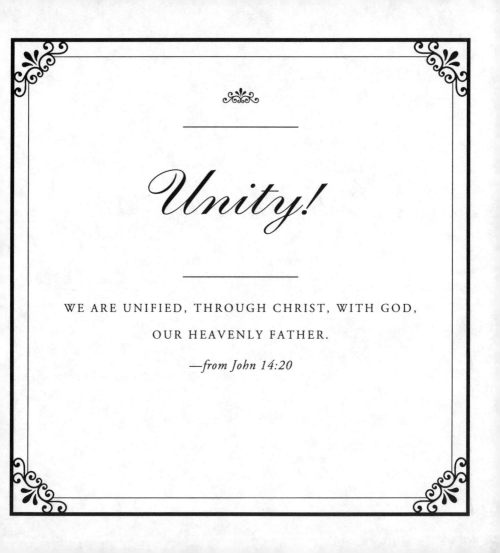

Unity!

WE ARE UNIFIED, THROUGH CHRIST, WITH GOD,

OUR HEAVENLY FATHER.

—from John 14:20

Fruitfulness!

IF YOU LIVE IN CHRIST AND ALLOW HIM TO
LIVE IN YOU, THEN YOU WILL
BE AS A BRANCH TO HIS VINE, AND HE WILL MAKE YOU
FRUITFUL AND BLESS
YOU WITH HIS GREAT GLORY.

—from John 15:4-8

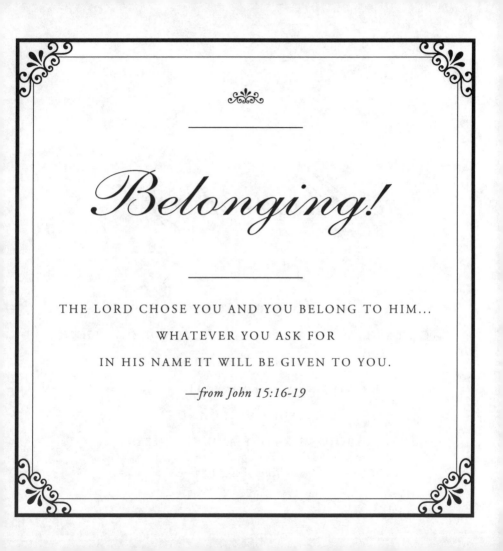

Belonging!

THE LORD CHOSE YOU AND YOU BELONG TO HIM…

WHATEVER YOU ASK FOR

IN HIS NAME IT WILL BE GIVEN TO YOU.

—from John 15:16-19

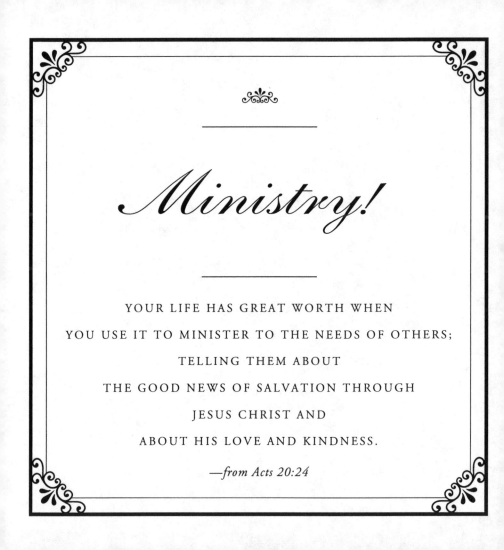

Ministry!

YOUR LIFE HAS GREAT WORTH WHEN
YOU USE IT TO MINISTER TO THE NEEDS OF OTHERS;
TELLING THEM ABOUT
THE GOOD NEWS OF SALVATION THROUGH
JESUS CHRIST AND
ABOUT HIS LOVE AND KINDNESS.

—from Acts 20:24

Inheritance!

YOU HAVE BEEN SET APART SO THAT
YOU MAY RECEIVE THE LORD'S FORGIVENESS AND
THE INHERITANCE HE HAS
SET ASIDE FOR EVERYONE WHO BELIEVES IN HIM.

—from Acts 26:18

Eternal Life!

GOD PROMISES ETERNAL LIFE TO EVERYONE

WHO DOES HIS WILL AND

WHO DESIRES NOTHING BEYOND AN ETERNITY

WITH HIM.

—*from Romans 2:7*

Righteousness!

YOU HAVE BEEN SET FREE FROM THE SLAVERY

OF SIN SO THAT YOU CAN

BECOME A SERVANT OF RIGHTEOUSNESS.

—from Romans 6:18

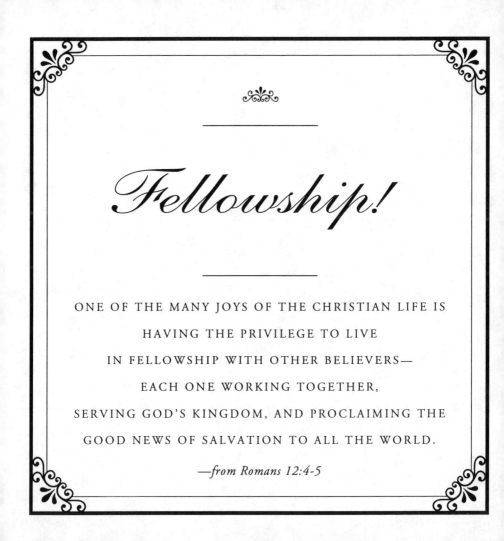

Fellowship!

ONE OF THE MANY JOYS OF THE CHRISTIAN LIFE IS

HAVING THE PRIVILEGE TO LIVE

IN FELLOWSHIP WITH OTHER BELIEVERS—

EACH ONE WORKING TOGETHER,

SERVING GOD'S KINGDOM, AND PROCLAIMING THE

GOOD NEWS OF SALVATION TO ALL THE WORLD.

—from Romans 12:4-5

Temperance!

IF YOU ASK THE LORD TO HELP YOU LIVE
A PURE AND HOLY LIFE, HE WILL
GIVE YOU A SPIRIT OF TEMPERANCE AND YOU WILL
BE ABLE TO RESIST TEMPTATION.

—from Romans 13:14

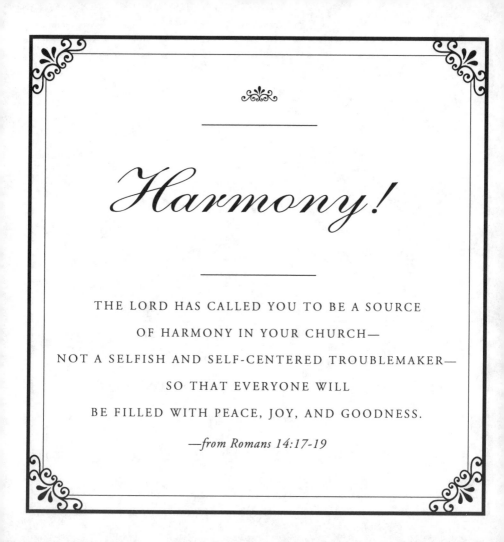

Harmony!

THE LORD HAS CALLED YOU TO BE A SOURCE

OF HARMONY IN YOUR CHURCH—

NOT A SELFISH AND SELF-CENTERED TROUBLEMAKER—

SO THAT EVERYONE WILL

BE FILLED WITH PEACE, JOY, AND GOODNESS.

—from Romans 14:17-19

Encouragement!

THE HOLY SPIRIT AND THE WORD OF GOD WERE
GIVEN TO CHRISTIANS SO THAT
WE CAN ENCOURAGE EACH OTHER AND TOGETHER
EAGERLY AWAIT THE TIME WHEN
THE LORD WILL RETURN TO PUT AN END TO ALL
SIN AND SUFFERING.

—from Romans 15:4-5

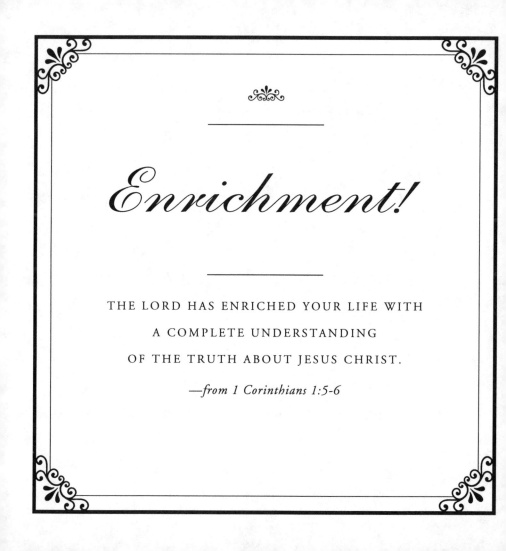

Enrichment!

THE LORD HAS ENRICHED YOUR LIFE WITH

A COMPLETE UNDERSTANDING

OF THE TRUTH ABOUT JESUS CHRIST.

—from 1 Corinthians 1:5-6

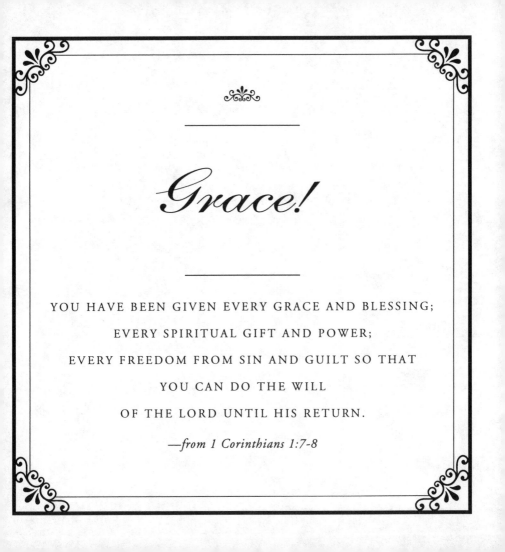

Grace!

YOU HAVE BEEN GIVEN EVERY GRACE AND BLESSING;

EVERY SPIRITUAL GIFT AND POWER;

EVERY FREEDOM FROM SIN AND GUILT SO THAT

YOU CAN DO THE WILL

OF THE LORD UNTIL HIS RETURN.

—from 1 Corinthians 1:7-8

Acceptance!

JESUS CHRIST PURCHASED YOUR SALVATION

WITH HIS BLOOD

SO THAT YOU COULD BE PURE AND HOLY

AND ACCEPTABLE BEFORE GOD.

—from 1 Corinthians 1:30

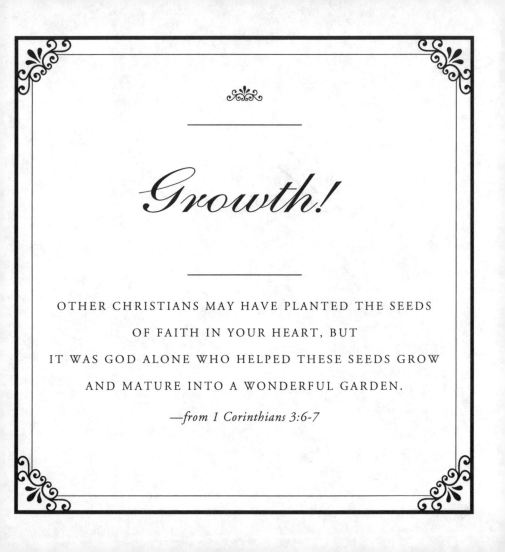

Growth!

OTHER CHRISTIANS MAY HAVE PLANTED THE SEEDS

OF FAITH IN YOUR HEART, BUT

IT WAS GOD ALONE WHO HELPED THESE SEEDS GROW

AND MATURE INTO A WONDERFUL GARDEN.

—from 1 Corinthians 3:6-7

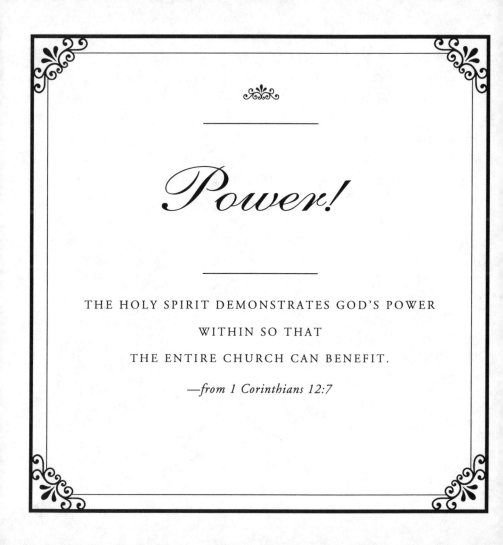

Power!

THE HOLY SPIRIT DEMONSTRATES GOD'S POWER

WITHIN SO THAT

THE ENTIRE CHURCH CAN BENEFIT.

—from 1 Corinthians 12:7

Victory!

YOU CAN BE CONFIDENT THAT THE LORD HAS

ALREADY WON THE VICTORY

OVER SIN AND DEATH SO THAT EVERYTHING

YOU DO FOR HIS KINGDOM

HAS GREAT VALUE AND IS NEVER WASTED.

—from 1 Corinthians 15:58

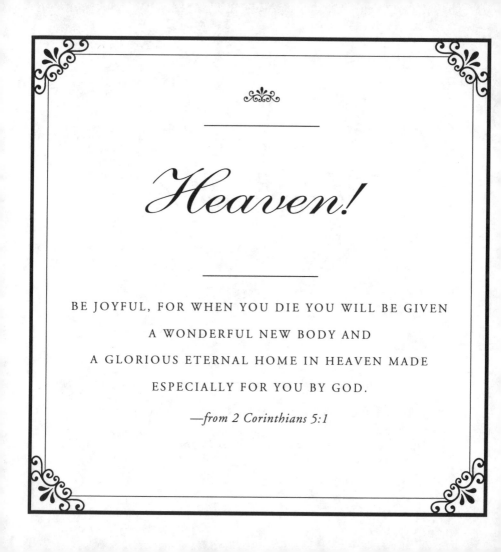

Heaven!

BE JOYFUL, FOR WHEN YOU DIE YOU WILL BE GIVEN

A WONDERFUL NEW BODY AND

A GLORIOUS ETERNAL HOME IN HEAVEN MADE

ESPECIALLY FOR YOU BY GOD.

—from 2 Corinthians 5:1

Endurance!

GOD GRACIOUSLY PROVIDES HIS PEOPLE WITH
THE ENDURANCE TO FACE THE
CHALLENGES, SUFFERING, AND HARDSHIPS OF LIFE.

—from 2 Corinthians 6:4

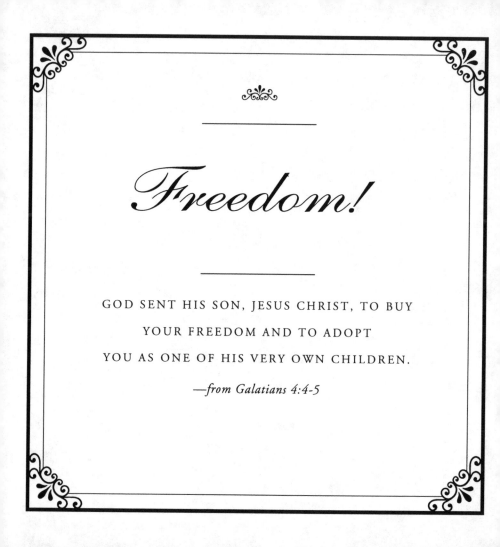

Freedom!

GOD SENT HIS SON, JESUS CHRIST, TO BUY
YOUR FREEDOM AND TO ADOPT
YOU AS ONE OF HIS VERY OWN CHILDREN.

—from Galatians 4:4-5

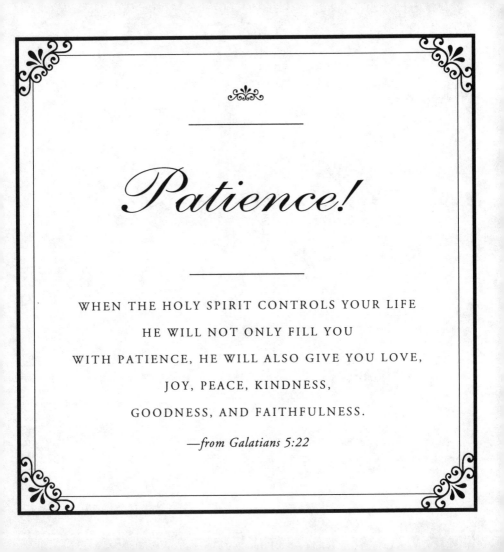

Patience!

WHEN THE HOLY SPIRIT CONTROLS YOUR LIFE
HE WILL NOT ONLY FILL YOU
WITH PATIENCE, HE WILL ALSO GIVE YOU LOVE,
JOY, PEACE, KINDNESS,
GOODNESS, AND FAITHFULNESS.

—from Galatians 5:22

Atonement!

GOD LOVED YOU SO MUCH THAT HE SENT
HIS SON TO DIE ON A CROSS
TO ATONE FOR YOUR SINS THROUGH THE
SPILLING OF HIS PRECIOUS BLOOD.

—from Ephesians 1:7

Trust!

THE ONLY RESPONSE YOU MUST OFFER GOD
FOR YOUR SALVATION IS TO TRUST IN HIM—AND,
IN HIS INFINITE MERCY AND LOVE,
HE WILL EVEN GIVE YOU THE ABILITY TO TRUST
THROUGH THE EMPOWERING
PRESENCE OF THE HOLY SPIRIT.

—from Ephesians 2:8

Welcome!

BECAUSE OF WHAT JESUS CHRIST DID ON
YOUR BEHALF, YOU ARE
WELCOME TO COME INTO THE LORD'S PRESENCE
AND ENJOY HIS COMPANY.

—from Ephesians 3:12

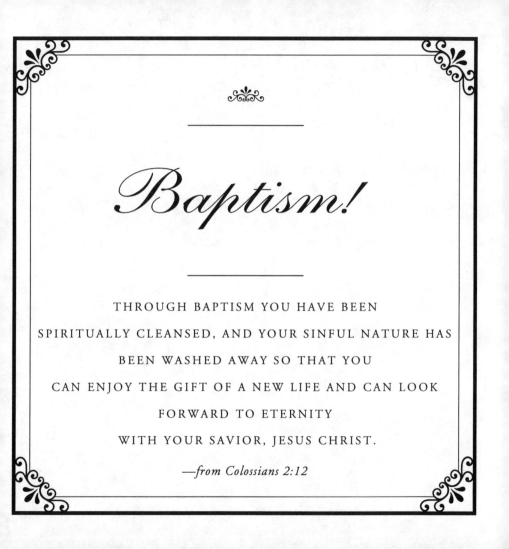

Baptism!

THROUGH BAPTISM YOU HAVE BEEN
SPIRITUALLY CLEANSED, AND YOUR SINFUL NATURE HAS
BEEN WASHED AWAY SO THAT YOU
CAN ENJOY THE GIFT OF A NEW LIFE AND CAN LOOK
FORWARD TO ETERNITY
WITH YOUR SAVIOR, JESUS CHRIST.

—from Colossians 2:12

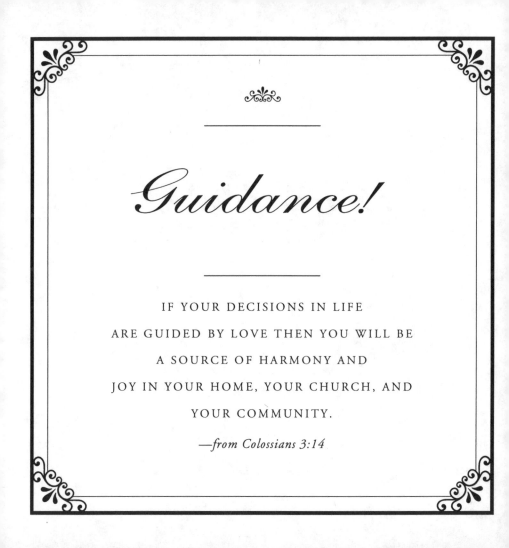

Guidance!

IF YOUR DECISIONS IN LIFE
ARE GUIDED BY LOVE THEN YOU WILL BE
A SOURCE OF HARMONY AND
JOY IN YOUR HOME, YOUR CHURCH, AND
YOUR COMMUNITY.

—from Colossians 3:14

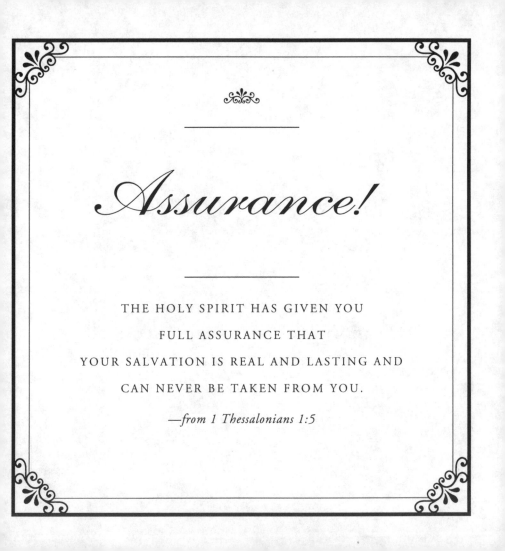

Assurance!

THE HOLY SPIRIT HAS GIVEN YOU
FULL ASSURANCE THAT
YOUR SALVATION IS REAL AND LASTING AND
CAN NEVER BE TAKEN FROM YOU.

—from 1 Thessalonians 1:5

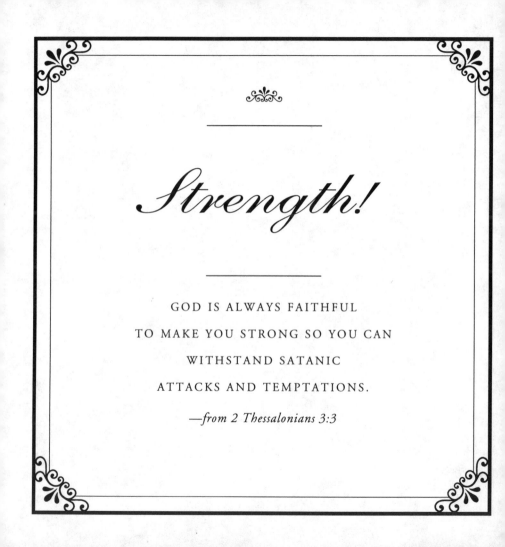

Strength!

GOD IS ALWAYS FAITHFUL

TO MAKE YOU STRONG SO YOU CAN

WITHSTAND SATANIC

ATTACKS AND TEMPTATIONS.

—from 2 Thessalonians 3:3

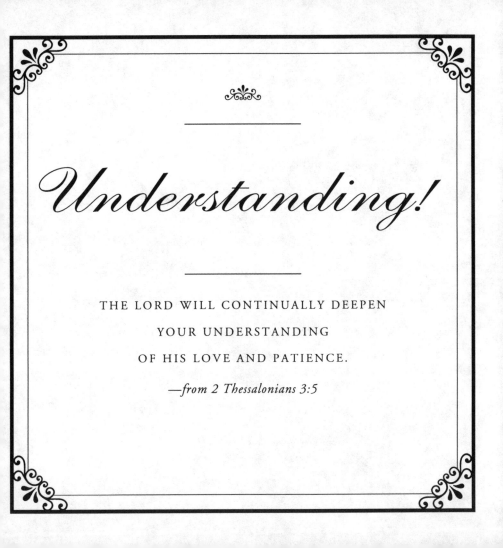

Understanding!

THE LORD WILL CONTINUALLY DEEPEN
YOUR UNDERSTANDING
OF HIS LOVE AND PATIENCE.

—from 2 Thessalonians 3:5

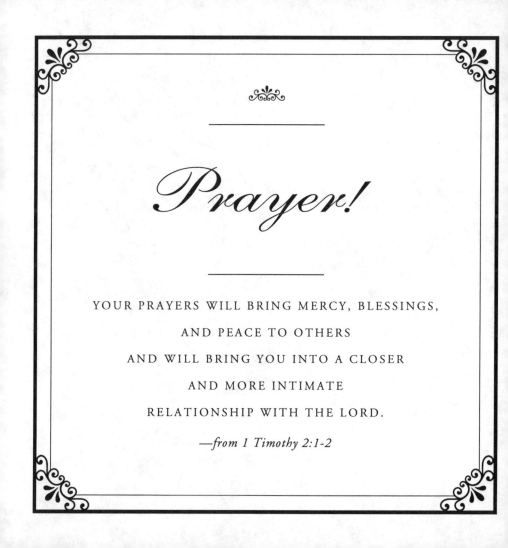

Prayer!

YOUR PRAYERS WILL BRING MERCY, BLESSINGS,

AND PEACE TO OTHERS

AND WILL BRING YOU INTO A CLOSER

AND MORE INTIMATE

RELATIONSHIP WITH THE LORD.

—from 1 Timothy 2:1-2

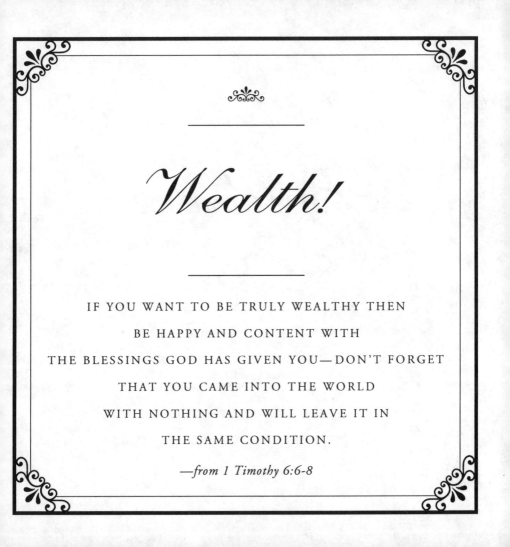

Wealth!

IF YOU WANT TO BE TRULY WEALTHY THEN

BE HAPPY AND CONTENT WITH

THE BLESSINGS GOD HAS GIVEN YOU—DON'T FORGET

THAT YOU CAME INTO THE WORLD

WITH NOTHING AND WILL LEAVE IT IN

THE SAME CONDITION.

—from 1 Timothy 6:6-8

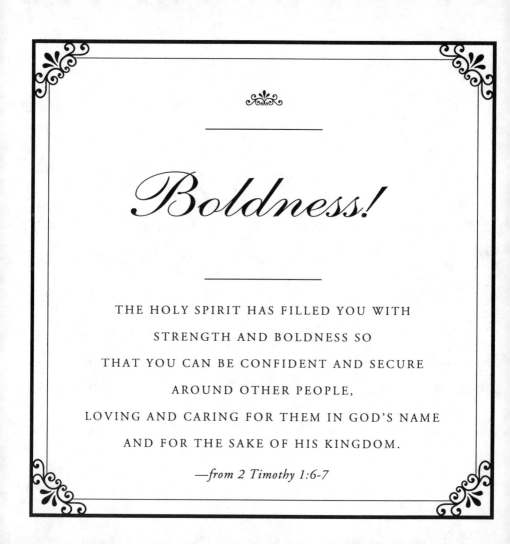

Boldness!

THE HOLY SPIRIT HAS FILLED YOU WITH
STRENGTH AND BOLDNESS SO
THAT YOU CAN BE CONFIDENT AND SECURE
AROUND OTHER PEOPLE,
LOVING AND CARING FOR THEM IN GOD'S NAME
AND FOR THE SAKE OF HIS KINGDOM.

—from 2 Timothy 1:6-7

Teaching!

COMMIT YOURSELF TO TEACHING

THE GREAT TRUTHS

OF GOD'S WORD TO THOSE WHO WILL LISTEN SO

THAT THEY, IN TURN,

CAN SHARE THEM WITH OTHERS.

—from 2 Timothy 2:2

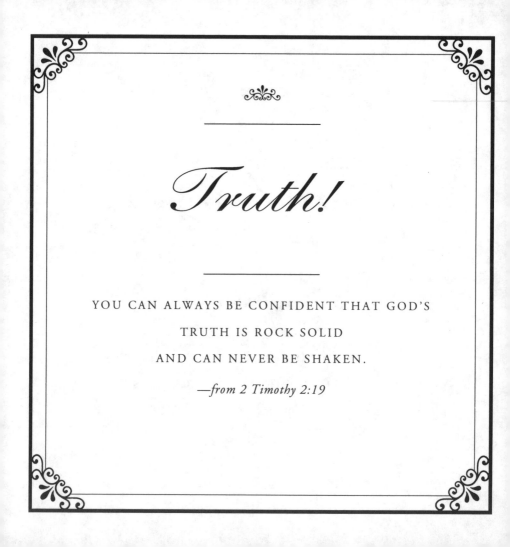

Truth!

YOU CAN ALWAYS BE CONFIDENT THAT GOD'S

TRUTH IS ROCK SOLID

AND CAN NEVER BE SHAKEN.

—from 2 Timothy 2:19

✦✦✦

Preparation!

THE WHOLE BIBLE HAS BEEN INSPIRED BY GOD
TO TEACH US WHAT IS TRUE AND TO MAKE US REALIZE
WHAT IS WRONG; TO STRAIGHTEN US OUT
AND HELP US DO WHAT IS RIGHT; AND TO PREPARE US
FOR EVERY SITUATION SO THAT WE CAN
ALWAYS TREAT THOSE AROUND US WITH LOVE.

—from 2 Timothy 3:16-17

Correction!

CORRECT AND REBUKE OTHERS WHEN
THEY NEED IT BUT REMEMBER TO ENCOURAGE THEM
TO DO WHAT IS RIGHT
ACCORDING TO GOD'S HOLY WORD.

—from 2 Timothy 4:2

Deliverance!

THE LORD IS FAITHFUL TO DELIVER YOU

FROM EVIL AND BRING YOU

SAFELY INTO HIS HEAVENLY KINGDOM.

—from 2 Timothy 4:18

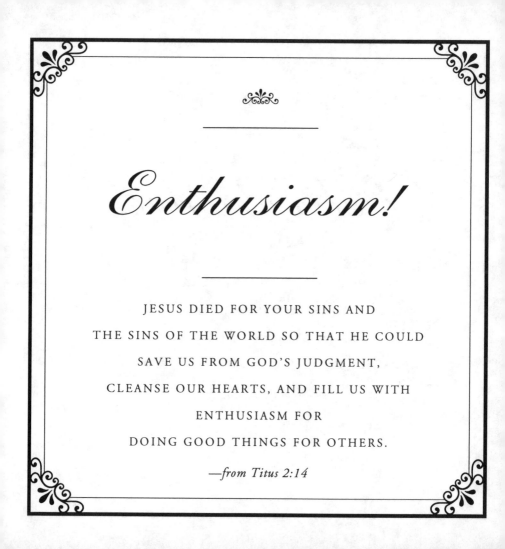

Enthusiasm!

JESUS DIED FOR YOUR SINS AND
THE SINS OF THE WORLD SO THAT HE COULD
SAVE US FROM GOD'S JUDGMENT,
CLEANSE OUR HEARTS, AND FILL US WITH
ENTHUSIASM FOR
DOING GOOD THINGS FOR OTHERS.

—from Titus 2:14

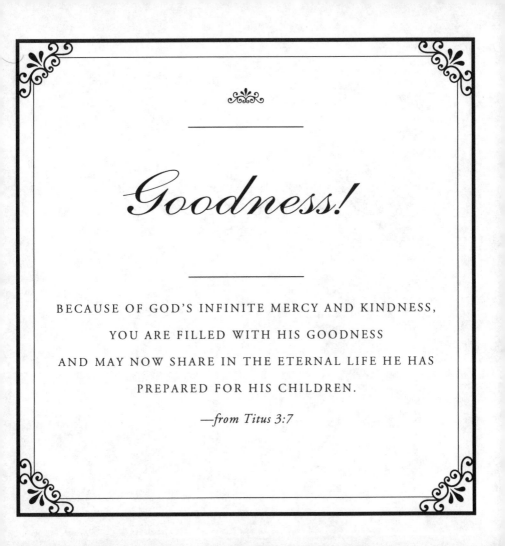

Goodness!

BECAUSE OF GOD'S INFINITE MERCY AND KINDNESS,

YOU ARE FILLED WITH HIS GOODNESS

AND MAY NOW SHARE IN THE ETERNAL LIFE HE HAS

PREPARED FOR HIS CHILDREN.

—from Titus 3:7

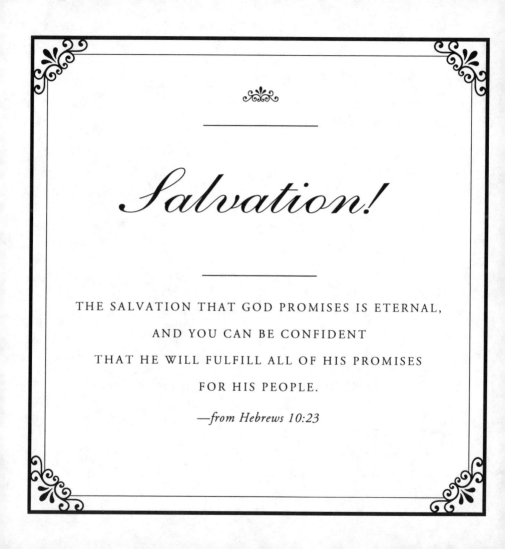

Salvation!

THE SALVATION THAT GOD PROMISES IS ETERNAL,

AND YOU CAN BE CONFIDENT

THAT HE WILL FULFILL ALL OF HIS PROMISES

FOR HIS PEOPLE.

—from Hebrews 10:23

Faith!

IT WAS FAITH THAT ENABLED ABEL TO OBEY GOD
AND OFFER A SACRIFICE PLEASING TO HIM,
AND IT IS FAITH THAT CONTINUES TO BE A SOURCE OF
ENCOURAGEMENT AND
GUIDANCE FOR BELIEVERS TODAY.

—from Hebrews 11:4

Satisfaction!

YOUR SATISFACTION AND SECURITY COME FROM GOD,

NOT MONEY OR POSSESSIONS,

AND HE HAS PROMISED THAT HE WILL "NEVER,

NEVER FAIL YOU NOR FORSAKE YOU."

—from Hebrews 13:5

Spiritual Strength!

SPIRITUAL STRENGTH IS A GIFT

FROM GOD AND DOES NOT COME BY FOLLOWING

CERTAIN RULES OR

EXPERIMENTING WITH STRANGE NEW IDEAS THAT

CONTRADICT HIS HOLY WORD.

—from Hebrews 13:9

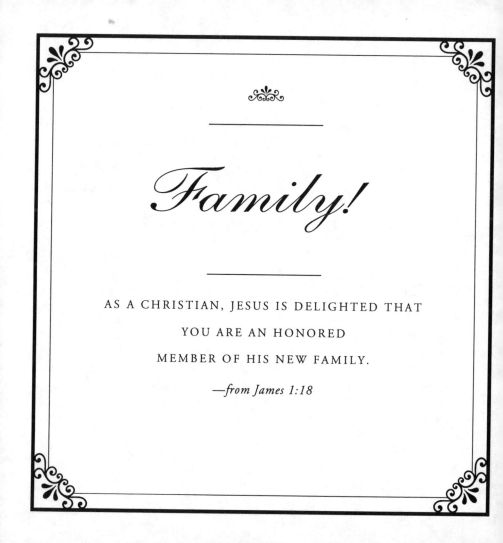

Family!

AS A CHRISTIAN, JESUS IS DELIGHTED THAT
YOU ARE AN HONORED
MEMBER OF HIS NEW FAMILY.

—from James 1:18

Diplomacy!

TO BE A DIPLOMAT YOU MUST BE
QUICK TO LISTEN,
SLOW TO SPEAK, AND WILLING TO CONTROL
YOUR TEMPER.

—from James 1:19

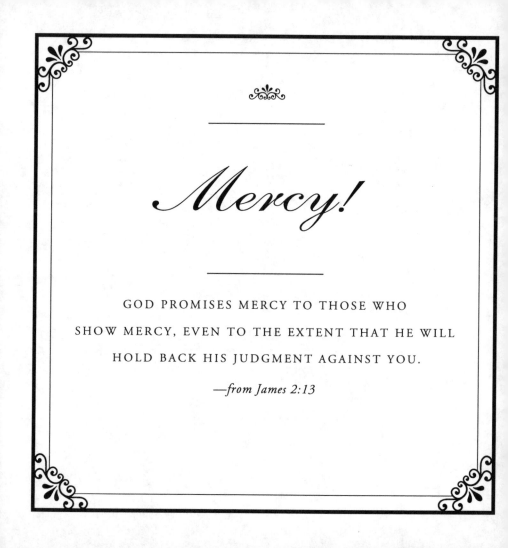

Mercy!

GOD PROMISES MERCY TO THOSE WHO
SHOW MERCY, EVEN TO THE EXTENT THAT HE WILL
HOLD BACK HIS JUDGMENT AGAINST YOU.

—from James 2:13

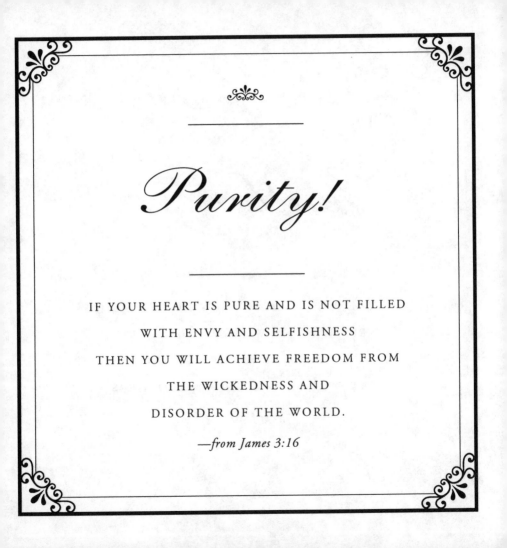

Purity!

IF YOUR HEART IS PURE AND IS NOT FILLED
WITH ENVY AND SELFISHNESS
THEN YOU WILL ACHIEVE FREEDOM FROM
THE WICKEDNESS AND
DISORDER OF THE WORLD.

—from James 3:16

Gentleness!

QUIET, MERCIFUL, PEACE-LOVING GENTLENESS

REFLECTS THE WISDOM OF HEAVEN

AND DEMONSTRATES A GENTLE AND SINCERE SPIRIT

THAT WILL BE A BLESSING TO OTHERS.

—*from James 3:17*

Beauty!

IF YOU ARE BEAUTIFUL WITHIN YOUR HEART,

THEN YOU WILL HAVE A

LASTING CHARM THAT IS PRECIOUS TO GOD AND

APPEALING TO THOSE AROUND YOU.

—from 1 Peter 3:4

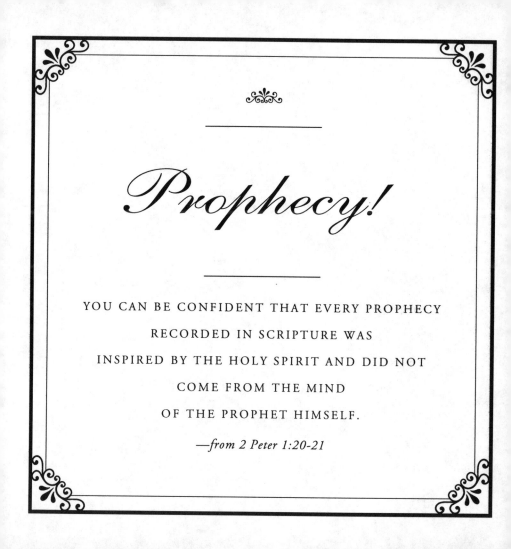

Prophecy!

YOU CAN BE CONFIDENT THAT EVERY PROPHECY

RECORDED IN SCRIPTURE WAS

INSPIRED BY THE HOLY SPIRIT AND DID NOT

COME FROM THE MIND

OF THE PROPHET HIMSELF.

—from 2 Peter 1:20-21

A Clear Conscience!

A CLEAR CONSCIENCE IS A WONDERFUL
BLESSING BECAUSE THEN YOU
WILL BE ABLE TO COME BEFORE THE LORD WITH
PEACE AND CONFIDENCE.

—from 1 John 3:21

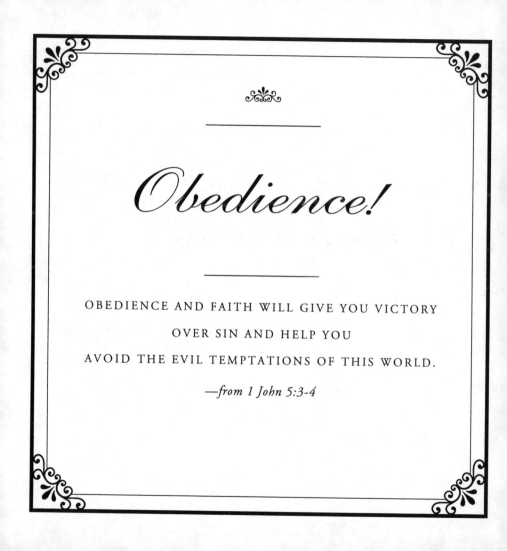

Obedience!

OBEDIENCE AND FAITH WILL GIVE YOU VICTORY

OVER SIN AND HELP YOU

AVOID THE EVIL TEMPTATIONS OF THIS WORLD.

—from 1 John 5:3-4

_____

Communion!

_____

JESUS LOVES YOU SO MUCH THAT HE WILL STAND
AT THE DOOR OF YOUR HEART,
PATIENTLY KNOCKING UNTIL YOU ASK HIM TO
COME IN AND ACCEPT HIS
COMMUNION AND FELLOWSHIP.

—*from Revelation 3:20*